82

Merry Christmas

to

Erika

from

the Hardings

the Joy of
CHRISTMAS

by
LEE THOMAS

CRESCENT

O Come all ye faithful,
Joyful and triumphant,
O come ye, O come ye to Bethlehem;
Come and behold Him,
Born the King of Angels:

O come, let us adore Him,
O come, let us adore Him,
O come, let us adore Him,
Christ the Lord!

Sing, choirs of Angels,
Sing in exultation,
Sing, all ye citizens of Heaven above:
"Glory to God
In the highest"

Anonymous: 18th Century.

Old Customs! Oh! I love the sound,
    However simple they may be:
Whate'er with time hath sanction found,
    Is welcome and is dear to me.
Pride grows above simplicity,
    And spurns them from her haughty mind
And soon the poet's song will be
    The only refuge they can find.

'December': John Cla

Thou day of happy sound and mirth,
    That long with childish memory stays,
How blest around the cottage hearth
    I met thee in my younger days!
Harping, with rapture's dreaming joys,
    On presents which thy coming found,
The welcome sight of little toys,
    The Christmas gift of cousins round:

'December': John Clare.

Out of the bosom of the air,
Out of the cloud-folds
   of her garments shaken,
Over the woodland brown and bare,
Over the harvest-fields forsaken,
Silent, and soft, and slow
Descends the snow.

'Snowflakes': Henry Wadsworth Longfellow.

The holly and the ivy,
When they are both full grown,
Of all the trees that are in the wood,
The holly bears the crown.

The rising of the sun,
And the running of the deer,
The playing of the merry organ,
Sweet singing in the choir.

The holly bears a blossom,
As white as lily flower;
And Mary bore sweet Jesus Christ,
To be our sweet Saviour.

The holly bears a berry,
As red as any blood,
And Mary bore sweet Jesus Christ
To do poor sinners good.

The holly bears a prickle,
As sharp as any thorn,
And Mary bore sweet Jesus Christ
On Christmas Day in the morn.

'The Holly and the Ivy': Traditional.

And behold the star which they had seen in the East, went before them until it came and stood over where the Child was. When they saw the star they rejoiced with exceeding great joy. Entering the house they found the Child with Mary, His mother, and fell down to worship Him. And opening their treasures, they offered Him gifts: gold, frankincense and myrrh.

Matthew 2:9-11.

I heard the bells on Christmas Day
Their old, familiar carols play,
      And wild and sweet
      The words repeat
Of peace on earth, good-will to men!

      Longfellow: 'Christmas Bells'.

What sweeter music can we bring
Than a carol, for to sing
The birth of this our heavenly King?
Awake the voice! Awake the string!
 We see Him come, and know Him ours,
 Who with His sunshine and His showers
 Turns all the patient ground to flowers.

'A Christmas Carol': Robert Herrick

Silent night, holy night
All is calm, all is bright
Round yon Virgin Mother and Child;
Holy Infant, so tender and mild,
Sleep in heavenly peace,
Sleep in heavenly peace.

Silent night, holy night,
Shepherds quake at the sight;
Glories stream from heaven afar,
Heavenly hosts sing alleluia.
Christ the Saviour is born,
Christ the Saviour is born.

Silent night, holy night,
Son of God, love's pure light;
Radiant beams from Thy holy face,
With the dawn of redeeming grace,
Jesus, Lord, at Thy birth,
Jesus, Lord, at Thy birth.

'Silent Night'.

Ring out, ye crystal spheres,
Once bless our human ears
(If ye have power to touch our senses so),
And let your silver chime
Move in melodious time,
And let the bass of heav'n's deep organ blow;
And with your ninefold harmony
Make up full consort to th'angelic symphony.

'On the Morning of Christ's Nativity': John Milton

At that time the angel Gabriel was sent from God into a city of Galilee, called Nazareth, to a virgin, espoused to a man whose name was Joseph, of the house of David, and the virgin's name was Mary.

Into her presence the angel came and said unto
her: Hail, thou who art full of grace; the Lord is
with thee; blessed art thou among women. She
was deeply troubled by what he said, and
wondered what this greeting might mean. Then
the angel said to her: Mary, do not be afraid; for
thou hast found grace with God: behold thou
shalt conceive in thy womb and shalt bear a son,
and thou shalt call him Jesus. He shall be great,
and shall be called the Son of the Most High, and
the Lord God shall give unto him the throne of
David His Father: and he shall reign in the house
of Jacob for ever, and of his kingdom there shall
be no end.

Luke 1:26-33.

Seraph quire singeth,
Angel bell ringeth:
Hark how they rime it,
Time it, and chime it.

Mid earth rejoices
Hearing such voices
Ne'ertofore so well
Carolling *Nowell*.

'Past Three O'Clock': Traditional.

In the bleak mid-winter
   Frosty wind made moan,
Earth stood hard as iron,
   Water like a stone;
Snow had fallen, snow on snow,
   Snow on snow,
In the bleak mid-winter
   Long ago.

What can I give Him,
   Poor as I am?
If I were a shepherd
   I would bring a lamb;
If I were a wise man
   I would do my part –
Yet what I can, I give Him,
   Give my heart.

'A Christmas Carol': Christina Rossetti.

You are the light of the world.
A city set on a hill cannot be hid. Nor
do men light a lamp and put it under a
bushel, but on a stand, and it gives light
to all in the house. Let your light so
shine before men, that they may see
your good works and give glory to your
Father who is in heaven.

Matthew 5:14-16.

No leaves are now upon the birch-tree there:
All now is stript to the cold wintry air.

See, not one tree but what has lost its leaves —
And yet the landscape wears a pleasing hue.
The winter chill on his cold bed receives
Foliage which once hung o'er the waters blue.

'The Winter's Come': John Clare

While shepherds watched their flocks by night,
All seated on the ground,
The angel of the Lord came down,
And glory shone around.

"Fear not", said he, for mighty dread
Had seized their troubled mind;
"Glad tidings of great joy I bring
To you and all mankind.

"To you in David's town this day
Is born of David's line
A Saviour who is Christ the Lord –
And this shall be the sign:

"The heavenly babe you there shall find
To human view displayed.
All meanly wrapped in swaddling bands
And in a manger laid.

"All glory be to God on high
And to the earth be peace:
Goodwill henceforth from heaven to men,
Begin and never cease."

'While Shepherds Watched their Flocks by Night':
Nahum Tate.

It came upon the midnight clear,
    That glorious song of old,
From angels bending near the earth
    To touch their harps of gold:
'Peace on the earth, good will to men,
    From heaven's all-gracious King!'
The world in solemn stillness lay
    To hear the angels sing.

'It came upon the Midnight Clear':
Edmund Hamilton Sears.

Hark! the herald angels sing,
Glory to the new-born King,
Peace on earth and mercy mild
God and sinners reconciled.
Joyful all ye nations rise,
Join the triumph of the skies;
With the Angelic host proclaim,
"Christ is born in Bethlehem".
Hark! the herald angels sing:
"Glory to the new-born King".

'Hark the Herald Angels Sing':
Charles Wesley.

Softly fell the snow that night
and made the earth a coverlet
of bright, white snow.

Boughs heavy with the weight of it
were powdered by a million flakes
of bright, white snow.

'Winter': Thomas Millford.

We three kings of Orient are;
Bearing gifts we traverse afar
Field and fountain, moor and mountain,
Following yonder star.

O Star of wonder, star of light
Star with royal beauty bright,
Westward leading, still proceeding,
Guide us to thy perfect light.

Glorious now, behold Him arise,
King, and God, and sacrifice!
Alleluia, Alleluia,
Earth to the heavens replies.

'We Three Kings': Dr John Henry Hopkins Jr.

Now, the tree is decorated with bright merriment, and song, and dance, and cheerfulness. And they are welcome. Innocent and welcome be they ever held beneath the branches of the Christmas Tree, which ca[s]t no gloomy shadow!

'A Christmas Tree': Charles Dickens

With holly and ivy,
So green and so gay,
We deck up our houses
As fresh as the day;
With bay and rosemary
And laurel complete;
And everyone now
Is a king in conceit.

'Welcome Christmas': Anonymous

Then entered in those Wise Men three,
Full reverently upon their knee,
And offered there, in His presence,
Their gold, and myrrh, and frankincense.

Nowell, Nowell, Nowell, Nowell,
Born is the King of Israel.

Then let us all with one accord,
Sing praises to our Heavenly Lord,
That hath made Heaven and earth of nought,
And with His blood mankind hath bought.

Nowell, Nowell, Nowell, Nowell,
Born is the King of Israel.

'The First Nowell': Traditional.

Christmas candles cast their warming light,
And joyful bells ring out their message clear
That long ago in Bethlehem's still night
A star foretold the infant's birth was near.

'A Christmas Carol': James MacMillan.

Away in a manger, no crib for a bed,
The little Lord Jesus lay down his sweet head,
The stars in the bright sky looked down where He lay,
The little Lord Jesus asleep on the hay.

The cattle are lowing, the Baby awakes,
But little Lord Jesus, no crying He makes,
I love Thee, Lord Jesus! Look down from the sky,
And stay by my side until morning is nigh.

Be near me, Lord Jesus; I ask Thee to stay
Close by me for ever, and love me I pray,
Bless all the dear children in Thy tender care,
And fit us for heaven to live with Thee there.

'Away in a Manger': Anonymous.

He brought light out of darkness, not out of a lesser light; he can bring thy summer out of winter, though thou have no spring; though in the ways of fortune, or understanding, or conscience, thou have been benighted till now, wintered and frozen, clouded and eclipsed, damped and benumbed, smothered and stupified till now, now God comes to thee, not as in the dawning of the day, not as in the bud of the spring, but as the sun at noon.

(From a Sermon at St Paul's, 1624): John Donne.

God be in my head,
  And in my understanding;
God be in my mouth,
  And in my speaking;
God be in my heart,
  And in my thinking.

Sarum Primer.

First published in 1979 by Colour Library International Ltd.
© Illustrations: Colour Library International (U.S.A.) Ltd, 163 East 64th Street, New York 10021.
Colour separations by Fercrom, Barcelona, Spain.
Display and text filmsetting by Focus Photoset, London, England.
Printed by ROSES, bound by EUROBINDER - Barcelona-Spain
Published by Crescent Books, a division of Crown Publishers Inc.
All rights reserved.
Library of Congress Catalogue Card No. 79-2323
CRESCENT 1979